Elizabeth Akers

The Silver Bridge and other Poems

Elizabeth Akers

The Silver Bridge and other Poems

ISBN/EAN: 9783743303560

Manufactured in Europe, USA, Canada, Australia, Japa

Cover: Foto ©Thomas Meinert / pixelio.de

Manufactured and distributed by brebook publishing software
(www.brebook.com)

Elizabeth Akers

The Silver Bridge and other Poems

THE SILVER BRIDGE

AND OTHER POEMS

BY

ELIZABETH AKERS

BOSTON AND NEW YORK
HOUGHTON, MIFFLIN AND COMPANY
The Riverside Press Cambridge
1886

CONTENTS.

		PAGE
THE SILVER BRIDGE		5
THE WILLOW		7
HER SPHERE		9
A WHITE ROSEBUD		13
IF I WERE DEAD		16
SPRING MIRACLES		19
HETERODOXY		21
AN EGYPTIAN LILY		23
IN SMITHFIELD		24
THE GRASS IS GREENER WHERE SHE SLEEPS		27
NIGHT AND MORNING		28
MY NEIGHBOR'S GARDEN		30
LOVE AND FRIENDSHIP		33
WHEN LILACS WAVE		35
SPRING-TIDE		36
DIVES AND THE ANGELS		38
DANDELION GHOSTS		42
LINES TO A TUSCAN AIR		45
AN OLD BATTLE-FIELD		47
A BIRTHDAY		49
THE MORNING OF THE YEAR		52
WINTER-KILLED		54

Day and Night 55
Kitty Cary 58
With Thee 60
A Pine Tree 62
True Motherhood 65
Inconstancy 67
Brier-Bloom 70
After the Storm 72
Victor 74
A Picture 77
Drought 79
In Peace 82
Lost Days 85
False and True 87
The Silent Battle 92
"Until Death" 94
Little Feet 96
The Magnolia Tree 99
"Hadst Thou been Here" 102
Hughenden 104
Time's Losses 105
Fire-Flies 108
A Winter Night 110
Advice 113
Years After 117
At Fourscore 119
The Voices of Spring 121
One of Three 123

THE SILVER BRIDGE.

THE sunset fades along the shore,
And faints behind yon rosy reach of sea;
Night falls again, but ah, no more,
No more, no more,
My love returns to me.
The lonely moon builds soft and slow
Her silver bridge across the main,
But him who sleeps the wave below
Love waits in vain —
Ah no, ah no,
He never comes again!

But while some night beside the sea
I watch, when sunset's red has ceased to burn,
That silver path, and sigh, "Ah me,
Ah me, ah me,
He never will return!"
If, on that bridge of rippling light,
His homeward feet should find their way,

I should not wonder at the sight,
But only say
" Ah, love, my love,
I knew you would not stay ! "

THE WILLOW.

O WILLOW, why forever weep
　　As one who mourns an endless wrong?
What hidden woe can lie so deep,
　　What utter grief can last so long,
　　　　O sighing willow?

The spring makes haste, with step elate,
　　Your life and beauty to renew;
She even bids the roses wait,
　　And gives her first sweet care to you,
　　　　- Beloved willow!

The welcome redbreast folds his wing,
　　To pour for you his freshest strain;
To you the earliest bluebirds sing
　　Till all your light stems thrill again,
　　　　Responsive willow!

The sparrow trills his wedding song
　　And trusts his tender brood to you;

Fair flowering vines, the summer long,
  With clasp and kiss your beauty woo,
    O lovely willow !

The sunshine drapes your limbs with light,
  The rain braids diamonds in your hair,
The breeze makes love to you at night,
  Yet still you droop, and still despair,
    O loyal willow !

Beneath your boughs, at fall of dew,
  By lovers' lips is softly told
The tale that all the ages through
  Has kept the world from growing old,
    O listening willow !

But still, though April's buds unfold,
  Or summer sets the earth aleaf,
Or autumn pranks your robes with gold,
  You sway and sigh in graceful grief,
    O brooding willow !

Mourn on forever, unconsoled,
  And keep your secret sacredly,
No heart in all the world can hold
  A sweeter grace than constancy,
    O faithful willow !

HER SPHERE.

No outward sign her angelhood revealed,
  Save that her eyes were wondrous mild and fair, —
The aureole round her forehead was concealed
  By the pale glory of her shining hair.

She bore the yoke and wore the name of wife
  To one who made her tenderness and grace
A mere convenience of his narrow life,
  And put a seraph in a servant's place.

She cheered his meagre hearth; she blessed and
      warmed
  His poverty, and met its harsh demands
With meek, unvarying patience, and performed
  Its menial tasks with stained and battered hands.

She nursed his children through their helpless years, —
  Gave them her strength, her youth, her beauty's
      prime,
Bore for them sore privation, toil and tears,
  Which made her old and tired before her time.

(9)

And when fierce fever smote him with its blight,
　　Her calm, consoling presence charmed his pain;
Through long and thankless watches, day and night,
　　Her fluttering fingers cooled his face like rain.

With soft magnetic touch and murmurs sweet,
　　She brought him sleep, and stilled his fretful moan,
And taught his flying pulses to repeat
　　The mild and moderate measure of her own.

She had an artist's quick perceptive eyes
　　For all the beautiful; a poet's heart
For every changing phase of earth and skies,
　　And all things fair in nature and in art.

She looked with all a woman's keen delight
　　On jewels rich, and dainty drapery,
Rare fabrics and soft hues, — the happy right
　　Of those more favored but less fair than she;

On pallid pearls, which glimmer cool and white,
　　Dimming proud foreheads with their purity;
On silks, which gleam and ripple in the light,
　　And shift and shimmer like the summer sea;

On gems, like drops by sudden sunlight kissed,
　　When fall the last large brilliants of the rain;

On laces, delicate as frozen mist
    Embroidering a winter window-pane :

Yet, near the throng of worldly butterflies
    She dwelt, a chrysalis, in homely brown;
With costly splendors flaunting in her eyes,
    She went her dull way in a gingham gown.

Hedged in by alien hearts, unloved, alone,
    With slender shoulders bowed beneath their load,
She trod the path that Fate had made her own,
    Nor met one kindred spirit on the road.

Slowly the years rolled onward ; and at last,
    When the bruised reed was broken, and her soul
Knew its sad term of earthly bondage past,
    And felt its nearness to the heavenly goal,

Then a strange gladness filled the tender eyes
    Which gazed afar beyond all grief and sin,
And seemed to see the gates of Paradise
    Unclosing for her feet to enter in.

Vainly the master she had served so long
    Clasped her worn hands, and with remorseful tears,
Cried, "Stay, oh, stay ! Forgive my bitter wrong ;
    Let me atone for all these dreary years ! "

Alas for heedless hearts and blinded sense !
  With what faint welcome and what meagre fare,
What mean subjections and small recompense,
  We entertain our angels unaware !

A WHITE ROSEBUD.

O ROSEBUD, white rosebud,
  Whence comes your summer smile,
When to and fro outside the snow
  Is drifting all the while?
The cold midwinter tempest roars,
  The garden is bereft;
In all the waste of out-of-doors
  You have no kindred left.

O rosebud, dear rosebud,
  I wonder if you dream
How much more fair and sweet you are
  Than summer roses seem?
A rose that blooms in winter air
  In grace and beauty grows
— Because so precious and so rare —
  A thousand times a rose.

O rosebud, fair rosebud,
  You grieve not that your prime

Of radiant bloom and rich perfume
  Has come in winter-time;
And should I deem it hard and wrong,
  And drop ungrateful tears,
If life's best joy should bloom among
  The snows of later years?

O rosebud, sweet rosebud,
  What happy secret lies
Deep in your heart, so shut apart
  From rude and curious eyes?
Some dear delight of soul or sense
  Must make its dwelling there,
Else wherefore does this odor thence
  Rise like a grateful prayer?

O rosebud, rare rosebud,
  Would that you might repeat
The dreams which rest within your breast
  And make your life so sweet!
'T were well if we sad mortals knew,
  Our days are so forlorn;
So many souls among us, too,
  Alas, are winter-born!

O rosebud, my rosebud,
  My heart is like to you,

Since hidden deep therein I keep
  A happy secret too.
Oh, listen! winter-time will flee,
  And spring will bless the air,
And birds will sing, and there will be
  White rosebuds everywhere!

IF I WERE DEAD.

If I were dead,
        Or fled
To some far shore unknown,
    And you were left
        Bereft,
To wander here alone, —

    How long would you
        Be true
To memory of mine?
    How soon Love's debt
        Forget,
And seek another shrine?

    What fairer eyes
        Would rise
Like day-stars on your soul?
    And whose sweet speech
        Would teach
Delight to follow dole?

(16)

What charm make brief
Your grief?
What tender ministry
Heal with soft art
The heart
That ached for loss of me?

It would be so,
I know; —
Men's love is like to this:
They hold the near
Most dear,
The absent scarcely miss.

Some other face
Will grace
Your home when I have flown,
And claim as bliss
The kiss
I prized as mine alone.

Oh, love and pain!
In vain
We long for utter truth.
It is at best
A jest,
A day-dream of our youth;

And many wives
    Whose lives
Have lacked no duteous grace,
Are, ere they die,
    Thrown by
For a more youthful face.

Ah, well she sleeps
    Who keeps
Her love till life's last eve ;
If *then* he range
    Or change,
Ghosts do not blush, nor grieve.

But stay awhile
    And smile,
And let me fancy yet
That Time's cold breath
    Nor Death
Could make you quite forget !

SPRING MIRACLES.

WHEN the icy heart of nature yearns
 Faintly in its wintry stupor deep,
And the prescient earth, half-conscious, turns
 Sunward, smiling in her frozen sleep, —

How do dull-brown tubers, which have lain
 In their darksome prison heaped away,
Know that spring entreats the world again,
 And begin their struggle towards the day?

No spring light has touched them where they lay,
 No spring warmth has reached them in their tomb,
Yet they sprout and yearn and reach alway
 Toward the distant goal of life and bloom.

Planted in the self-same garden bed,
 Nourished by the self-same rain and light,
Whence do roses draw their glowing red?
 Whence the lily-cups their shining white?

(19)

Whence does the refulgent marigold
   Gain the gilding for her yellow globes?
Where do pansies find, amid the mould,
   Purple hues to prank their velvet robes?

How do sweet-peas plume their wings with pink,
   Lavender, and crimson rich and fair?
Nature gives them one and all to drink
   Limpid crystal, colorless as air.

Little gardener, with your golden locks
   Bright with sunshine or uncurled with dew,
Musing there among your pinks and phlox,
   Finding always something strange or new, —

Trust me, child, the wisest, strongest brain,
   Cobwebbed with much learning though it be,
Querying thus, must query all in vain,
   Pausing foiled at last, like you or me.

Sages ponder on the mysteries
   Hidden close in petal, root, and stem;
Nature yields more questions than replies, —
   Babes may ask, but who can answer them?

PRAY thee, put the sermon by, — vex my soul no
    more with creeds,
And the vague and slow rewards dealt to good and
    evil deeds ;
I am tired of differing sects, with their various
    bigotry, —
Ah, for me death holds no terror but the fear of
    losing thee !

In a heaven apart from thee, could my exiled soul
    rejoice ?
Could I join the angels' song, missing thence thy
    tender voice ?
What to me were gates of pearl, if they parted thee
    and me ?
What the streets so fair and golden, if I wandered
    lacking thee ?

What to me would be the joys of that bright and
    wondrous land,
If among them all I sought vainly for thy loving
    hand ?

What to me were pastures green, where thy feet
    could never be ?
Or the paths beside still waters, if thou walkedst not
    with me ?

Ah, wherever after death my still faithful soul may
    dwell, —
Saints may call it bliss or woe, they may name it
    heaven or hell, —
By thee only, O beloved, will my joy or pain be
    wrought,
I shall find my heaven beside thee, or my hell where
    thou art not !

AN EGYPTIAN LILY.

An arrowy point divides the oozy mould,
  A slender shaft, an emerald spear in rest;
  And soon another crowds the earliest,
Crumpled and crimped with creases manifold,
So closely were its swaddling-garments rolled, —
  Even as a baby's cheek, in slumber pressed
  Against the pillow of its downy nest,
Is stamped and dimpled by a careless fold.
  A faint green bud appears, and, hour by hour,
  Greatens and whitens; yet a little while,
And, marvelling, the gazer's eyes behold
  The fragrant glory of the perfect flower,
  Full of the magic of the mystic Nile, —
A wondrous cream-white trumpet, spiked with gold!

IN SMITHFIELD.

HERE on the very spot where now I stand
 Tracing on this gray stone the carvéd letters,
In other days a flame-crowned martyr band
 Stood slowly burning in their red-hot fetters,

Lapped by red tongues of flame, and choked with
  smoke,
 Under this very sky that frowns and lowers ;
Yet from the clouds no voice of thunder spoke,
 Nor tender mercy fell in quenching showers.

And so they died ; strong in the high belief
 That faithful ages would repeat their story,
That God would recompense their anguish brief,
 And crown their pain with everlasting glory.

The times have changed : not now does bigotry
 Heap funeral pyres in London's market-places,
Nor drag condemned enthusiasts out to die,
 With dawning haloes round their pallid faces ;

No holy bishop stands, with fierce intent,
  The smouldering fagots with his crosier turning,
And snuffs up, like a rose's breath, the scent
  Of wicked human thews and sinews burning.

We say these cruel evils brought forth good, —
  This age is more humane; nor is our boasting
A thing of mere conceit and hardihood, —
  We starve our martyrs now, instead of roasting.

All up and down this grim and haunted square
  They swarm, the martyrs of this age enlightened :
Children with feet and shoulders thin and bare ;
  Men with ignoble heads untimely whitened,

And faces blear and old before their time ;
  Lost girls, who earn their bread by smiles and
      laughter
Shameless and false as those who buy their crime, —
  Hating the present, dreading the hereafter ;

Youths old in guilt before their middle age,
  Schooled from their birth in words and deeds
      unholy ;
And toil-bent women-slaves, whose scanty wage
  Only enables them to starve more slowly ;

Mothers, who once, perhaps, knew love and mirth,
    When life was easier and their hearts were younger,
Now maddened by that dreariest sound on earth, —
    The cry of babes who wail with cold and hunger.

No aureole gathers round these grimy brows,
    No lofty faith upbears their load of trial,
No angel form above their torment bows;
    But want, and sin, and shame, and grim denial

Attend their rising up and lying down,
    And make them cringe, and steal, and lie, and
        grovel;
They win no martyr's fame, nor palm, nor crown,
    But die of vice and misery, in a hovel.

Ragged and hungry, comfortless and cold,
    Shivering and purple in the wintry breezes,
Which would they choose, knew they the story old,
    The age which burned, or this which starves and
        freezes?

London, England.

THE GRASS IS GREENER WHERE SHE SLEEPS.

THE grass is greener where she sleeps,
    The birds sing softlier there,
And Nature fondest vigil keeps
    Above a face so fair, —
For she was innocent and sweet
    As mortal thing can be, —
The only heart that ever beat,
    That beat alone for me.

To me her dearest thoughts were told,
    Her sweetest carols sung;
To her my love was never old,
    My face was always young.
Ah, life seems drear and little worth,
    Since she has ceased to be, —
The only heart in all the earth
    That never loved but me!

(27)

NIGHT AND MORNING.

I PAUSE beside the darkening pane,
  With homesick heart and weary hand,
To watch the fair day die again,
And evening with its shadowy train
  Creep slow along the lonesome land.

The west has lost its line of gold ;
  The clouds hang threatening, near and far,
Heavy and hopeless, fold on fold ;
And night comes moaning, unconsoled
  By glimmer of a single star.

Ah, why does hope depart with light ?
  And why do griefs and fears alway,
And bitter thoughts of loss and blight,
Come crowding back again with night,
  Like evil things which fear the day ?

Yet none but feeble souls complain ;
  The world is only dark, not lost ;
The day will shine on wave and plain,

(28)

The grass and flowers will spring again,
   Despite the night, despite the frost.

And when the east, like some far shore
   Of promise, broadens rosy-bright,
Visions of darkness vex no more,
For all their legions flee before
   The level lances of the light.

The grief that seemed too hard to bear,
   The thought which stung to sharpest pain,
Fade in the rich and golden air ;
The heart grows calm, the world grows fair,
   And life is sweet and dear again.

MY NEIGHBOR'S GARDEN.

Up to the border of my small domain
   My neighbor's garden stretches wide and sweet;
His roses toss against my window-pane;
   His jasmine wreathes my porch and doorway seat.

My threshold every May is carpeted
   With pale pink petals from his peach-tree blown;
His tallest lilac lifts its plumy head
   Up to the casement where I sit alone.

Waking I hear, as dawns the morning light, —
   My neighbor busy in his bordered walks,
Noting the added beauties born of night,
   Pulling the weeds among his flower-stalks.

From early March, when the brave crocus comes,
   Edging the beds with lines of blue and gold,
Till the consoling, kind chrysanthemums
   Contend against the winter's cruel cold, —

My neighbor toils with wise and patient hand,
   Scarce pausing in his work for sun or shower,

(30)

Evolving gradually from mould and sand
  The germ, the leaf, the perfect bud and flower.

A rare magician he, whose touch transmutes
  — Helped by the sprites which rule the airs and
    dews —   ·
Dry dormant seeds and dark unlovely roots
  To graceful shapes and richest scents and hues.

His garden teems with glad and brilliant lives ;
  There wheel and dive the gauzy dragon-flies,
Bees gather tribute for their distant hives,
  And gray moths flutter as the daylight dies.

Sparrows and wrens sing songs which need no words ;
  And over flower-cups scarce more bright than they,
Green-winged and scarlet-throated humming-birds
  Hang, tranced with sweet, then whir and dart
    away.

From branch to branch, beneath my watching eyes,
  His net a black-and-golden spider weaves,
And scores of many-colored butterflies
  Waltz in and out among the dancing leaves.

My neighbor in their midst — thrice-favored one !
  Delves, plants, trains, weeds, and waters patiently,

Studies the alchemy of rain and sun,
   And works his floral miracles for me.

For me ! not one enjoys this paradise
   As I, within my overlooking room ;
It is not seen, even by the owner's eyes,
   At once — the whole wide stretch of growth and
     bloom.

With sight and mind absorbed, he little thinks
   How all his garden's sweetness drifts to me ;
How his rich lilies and his spicy pinks
   Send incense up to me continually.

Yet still he labors faithfully and long
   My loneliness to brighten and beguile,
Asking for all this fragrance, bloom, and song
   Not even the small repayment of a smile.

Unconscious friend, who thus enrichest me,
   Long may thy darlings thrive, untouched by blight,
Unplagued by worm or frost ; and may there be
   No serpent in thine Eden of delight.

And ye whose spirits faint with weariness,
   Count not your work unvalued and unknown ;
Cheered by your toil, some silent soul may bless
   The hand that strives not for itself alone.

LOVE AND FRIENDSHIP.

I DREAMED I had for months been dead;
   Spring rain, and summer light and bloom
Had swept across my lonesome bed,
   With clover scent and wild bees' boom
   Lightening the place of half its gloom.

Serene and calm, my quiet ghost
   Came softly back to see the place
Where I had joyed and suffered most;
   To look upon his grieving face
   Whose memory death could not erase.

But he, my love, whom even in heaven
   I yearned to comfort and sustain,
Knowing how sore his heart was riven —
   My love, with life so changed to pain
   That he could never love again —

Forgetful of the golden band
   On my dead finger slumbering,
Now bent above another hand,

(33)

And clasped and kissed the dainty thing,
    And whispered of another ring.

Alas, poor ghost!   I felt a thrill,
    A sudden stab of mortal pain,
And sighed.   He shivered : " Ah, how chill
    The air has grown, and full of rain ;
    My darling, kiss me warm again ! "

Why should I linger ?   As I passed
    Her lips touched shyly, murmuring low,
Just where my own had kissed their last,
    Only so little while ago ;
    " Ah, well," I said, " 't is better so."

But one who in my life passed by
    With friendship's coolest touch and tone,
I found beneath the darkening sky,
    Beside my grave all bramble-grown,
    With sorrow in his eyes — alone.

A tear, down-glittering as he stood,
    Hung, star-like, in the grass below :
I blessed him in my gratitude —
    He smiled : " Dear heart, if she could know
    How sweet these brier-blossoms grow ! "

WHEN LILACS WAVE.

When lilacs wave their plumes in purple pride,
And dandelions star the country side,
 And the trim catbird, in her garrulous quest,
 Seeks straws and feathers for her careless nest,
Which seemingly she does not try to hide —

The redbreast's songs are jubilant and sweet,
The tender grass is velvet to the feet,
 And nightmare Care sits lightlier on the breast,
  When lilacs wave.

The almond swings its wands of rosy-white,
The scarlet tulips trim their torches bright,
 The crocuses, in gold and purple drest,
 Wake, fresh and perfect, from their winter rest —
And love is heaven, and life is all delight,
  When lilacs wave.

(35)

SPRING-TIDE.

THE cherry-tree is clad in white
  As though with clinging snow,
The peach is pink with blossoming,
  The red-fringed maples glow,
And brightly on the sunnier slopes
  The grass begins to grow.

The climbing rose-briers teem with buds,
  And flaunt their promise high ;
The strawberry-blossom lifts again
  Its white-and-golden eye,
And herb and weed, through damp dead leaves,
  Crowd up to see the sky.

The grape rejects the last year's bond
  Which cramped its wandering will,
The clambering vine forgets the hand
  That nailed it to the sill,
And tendril, stem, and velvet leaf
  Shoot upward, upward still.

(36)

And all the dead year's woes and wrongs,
   The heat and dust and din
Of summer-time — the bitter winds
   Which winter ushered in,
Are now, amid this fresh new life,
   As though they had not been.

How sweet to cast aside the load
   Which time and sorrow bring,
The galling bonds, the outgrown ties,
   The griefs which gnaw and cling,
And build a fresh and perfect life
   Anew with every spring —

With last year's dead leaves cast aside,
   And last year's chains unbound,
To leave the husks of age and care
   Behind us in the ground,
And rise into the gracious light,
   With youth and gladness crowned !

DIVES AND THE ANGEL.

An angel came to Dives as he slept,
    A Presence with severe and searching glance,
Who stooped and questioned him. " How have you
        kept
    The promise of your rich inheritance ?

"How is it that you still join field to field,
    And house to house, and make your treasure more,
While want and misery remain unhealed,
    And wretched children beg from door to door ?

·" While pallid women, finer-souled than you,
    Drudge weary year on year for scantiest wage,
No hope before them, all the long days through,
    But toil in youth and beggary in age ?

" Has Heaven, which dowered you as its almoner,
    Found you a faithful servant, just and true ?
How many hearts, with gratitude astir,
    Are happier to-day because of you ? "

(38)

"Hear, Lord!" replied the rich man, "I implore!
  I know my wealth is only shining dust;
I turn no homeless beggar from my door
  Without a cup of water and a crust.

"To bring the heathen to thy feet more near,
  My name is foremost, and my aid is sure,
And my discarded garments, year by year,
  Console the shivering shoulders of thy poor."

"Unfaithful steward! false and self-confessed,
  Who hope to win the favor of the skies
By grasping and enjoying all the best,
  And giving only what you do not prize!

"You make a virtue of your selfishness
  And hold the joy of giving poor and cheap,
By offering to another's sore distress
  That which you do not want and would not keep!

"The work-girl who divides her scanty store
  With one more poor, is princelier far than you —
A penny from her slender purse is more
  Than thousands from your bounteous revenue.

"Your fortunate fingers hold the golden keys
  Which make it a delight and joy to live;

The jewelled gates of luxury and ease
  Swing wide, and yield you all that life can give.

" You dwell within a palace grand and proud,
  Fair as though conjured by a wizard's spell,
While others wander shelterless, or crowd
  In wretched huts where beasts would scorn to
    dwell.

" You clothe yourself in raiment rich and fine,
  And toss your brother garments coarse and old ;
You give the water, and withhold the wine,
  Divide the copper, and retain the gold.

" Is it because you earn reward and praise
  By purer heart and life, and nobler deeds,
That you walk daintily life's lilied ways,
  While he goes stumbling in its thorns and weeds ?

" What is it that you fling the poor a crust
  While you fare delicately every day ?
What is it that you give because you must
  And still live on in wealth because you may ?

" Then, when at last Death's chill compelling clutch
  Has pinched your grasping fingers numb and cold,
You try to gain the praise you crave so much
  By scattering what you cannot longer hold.

" The selfish worm within the apple's core,
  Which revels all his life in fruit or flower,
Who thanks him, that when he can eat no more
  He leaves behind what he could not devour?

" Is it your virtue, then, that you forsake
  The precious gold of which you are so fond?
You leave it only that you cannot take
  A credit-letter on the world beyond.

" Beware ! for noting all your narrow greeds,
  An eye which cannot err and does not sleep
Will scan, as measure of your generous deeds,
  Not only what you give — but what you keep ! "

DANDELION GHOSTS.

THE dooryard flower that children love
All other common flowers above,
The dandelion-bloom, alas,
No longer stars the roadside grass,
But folds away its yellow robes;
And now from countless gauzy globes,
Gray gossamer ghosts float everywhere,
Like bubbles blown along the air.

Dear homelike flower, which cheers alway
The dusty path of every day,
Even death is kind to thee, and brings
Twin-gifts of liberty and wings;
O, peer of butterflies and bees,
Fair playmate of the wandering breeze,
Methinks I would rejoice to be
A free and fetterless ghost like thee!

No ghastly phantom, pale and stark,
Stalking, reproachful, through the dark,

To fright the souls which held me dear,
And mourned my loss with tear on tear; —
And yet, at last — so hard to bear
Are loneliness and dull despair —
Their pain of sore bereavement healed
With love more warm than ghosts can yield; —

No spectre, bringing fear and dread,
To blanch from timid lips the red,
But such a gentle ghost as might
Unchallenged come in fair daylight,
Unsoiled by dust, unwet by dew,
In fearless freedom strange and new,
To sail serenely through the air
Uncaught, unhindered, everywhere.

No fate were happier than to be
An evanescent ghost like thee,
A mild returner from the dead,
Which few would note, and none would dread;
To visit, not in grief or gloom,
The scenes which saw my early bloom,
And mark how perfect and how fair
The world could be, — and I not there!

Ah, happy flower, that smilest through
Thy three bright days of sun and dew,

And then, when time decrees thy doom,
Risest anew in rarer bloom,
A perfect sphere of daintiest white,
As soft as air, as still as light,
Leaving these earthly damps of ours
To seek, perhaps, the heaven of flowers!

LINES TO A TUSCAN AIR.

My heart has learned a simple song,
　More sweet than summer birds' —
Its burden lasts the whole day long,
　Though few and brief the words ;
And thus in sun and shadow,
　I sing it o'er and o'er —
　　"My love! my love!
　My love forevermore!"

The golden light may leave the sky,
　The gloomy clouds may frown —
The flowers may close, the winds may cry,
　The mournful rain come down ;
Yet though the tempests gather,
　I carol as before —
　　"My love! my love!
　My love forevermore!"

And years may pass and youth may go,
　And morning dreams depart,
And time may bring me care and woe,
　It cannot break my heart —

(45)

In life or death exulting,
My joy I still outpour —
" My love! my love!
My love forevermore!"

AN OLD BATTLE-FIELD.

THIS fair broad stretch of level grass,
   Spangled with bee and bloom and bud,
A few short years ago, alas,
   Was one wide waste of death and blood.

Here boomed the cannon's thunderous roar,
   And strong arms strove, and brave hearts bled; —
The sickened earth was dark with gore,
   And heaped and cumbered with the dead.

But now, how different! Tender notes
   Of love and gladness fill the air,
The mocking-birds' melodious throats
   Bubble with music everywhere;

The wild plants blossom as of old,
   Before the world had ever sinned;
The pink azalea's buds unfold
   And sweeten every wandering wind;

The strawberry-bloom's clear whiteness shows
   No red remembrance of a stain,

Although the sod whereon it grows
　　Was deluged once with crimson rain.

And daily on the slope's green breast
　　The tribes of blossoming things increase —
But dearer far than all the rest
　　The fair white flower whose name is Peace —

Whose gracious leaves to heal the ills
　　Which sapped the nation's life are sent —
Whose fragrance blesses all the hills —
　　Whose fruits are plenty and content.

As some wise mother's tender thought
　　Forgives her children's angry strife,
Conceals the wrong their wrath has wrought,
　　And builds thereon a gentler life ;

So Nature's great maternal soul
　　Forgives the petty wars of men, —
Forgets the battle's awful roll,
　　And bids the bluebird sing again ;

And from the trampled sod, restored
　　By summer rain and winter snow,
Blots out the track of fire and sword,
　　And makes the purple violets grow.

Richmond, Virginia.

A BIRTHDAY.

Now when the landscape lies all hushed and stilly
    Beneath the cold gray sky and shrouding snow,
Dawns the dim birthday, shadowy and chilly,
Of my sweet winter-child — my rare white lily,
    Loved all too well, and lost so long ago.

Sometimes I marvel, dazed by doubt and distance,
    Whether she was a mortal baby fair
Or some more glorified and pure existence
Lent for a little — a divine assistance
    To help me over uttermost despair.

I bring to other birthdays kiss and token,
    And loving wishes crowding fond and fast —
To this I only bring a woe unspoken,
Bitter rebellious tears, a heart half broken,
    Bruising itself against the cruel past.

Year after year I think of her as older,
    And muse upon her growth, and softly speak;
Now without stooping I could clasp and hold her, —

And now her golden head would reach my shoul-
    der, —
  And now her sweet white brow would touch my
    cheek.

Would earthly years have had the power to render
  That holy face less innocent and fair?
And those clear eyes, so luminous and tender,
Would they have kept undimmed their depths of
    splendor,
  Amid these heavy clouds of grief and care?

I wonder, when I see my locks grown duller
  By blighting years, and streaked with silvery
    strands,
If her bright hair has still the sun-warm color
It wore when on my breast I used to lull her,
  Smoothing its shining waves with loving hands.

While time has aged and saddened me so greatly,
  Has she outgrown each changing childish mood?
By the still waters does she walk sedately
A tall and radiant spirit, fair and stately,
  In the full prime of perfect angelhood?

In that far dwelling, where I cannot reach her,
  Has she who was so fragile and so sweet, —

An untaught babe, a tender little creature, —
Grown wise enough to be my guide and teacher,
  And will her presence awe me when we meet?

Oh, if her baby face has waxed no older,
  Or if to angel stature she has grown —
Whether as child or woman I behold her,
With what wild rapture will these arms enfold her —
  This longing heart reclaim her for its own!

THE MORNING OF THE YEAR.

A TENDER music, new and rare,
  Breaks up the songless silences, —
The voice of the entreating air
  Soliciting the leafless trees.

" Awake," it calls — " O bashful buds,
  The prelude of the birds is here, —
The sunlight falls in gracious floods,
  It is the morning of the year !

" The lily-bulbs, unfearing, sprout
  Along the garden-border's edge,
While peach trees stand in blushing doubt,
  And half distrust spring's timid pledge ;

" The sparrow, constant evermore,
  Begins anew his insect-quest,
The wren, beside the open door,
  Peers curious at her last year's nest —

" The bluebird tunes his bravest lay
  And fills the morn with sudden trills,

(52)

Soft lines of greenness mark the way
  Of watercourses down the hills —

"Awake, dull world, and cast aside
  The mouldy robes of age and care,
Put on thy Eden-youth and pride —
  Be glad again, and strong, and fair !

"Awake, awake, O drowsy buds —
  The prelude of the birds is here,
The sunlight falls in tender floods,
  It is the morning of the year ! "

WINTER-KILLED.

Beneath the snow the roses sleep,
Below the wave the pearls lie deep —
   Wedged in the rock-rift, centuries old,
   Lie yellow veins of virgin gold;
Ice-locked within the forest nook,
Sleeps the bright spirit of the brook,
   And under more than wintry fate
   Or ocean's depths or boulder's weight,
Or fettering ice or frozen grass,
Dishonored love lies dead, alas!

Yet spring shall wake the rose once more,
The diver bring the pearl to shore,
   With sturdy toil the miner bold
   Shall blast the rock and glean the gold;
And April set the brooklet free
To seek its waiting bride, the sea, —
   But not spring's vivifying kiss,
   Nor summer rain's persuasiveness,
Nor toil, nor search, nor patient pain,
Can bring dead love to life again!

(54)

DAY AND NIGHT.

ERE wholly fails the waning light,
   The moon, amid heaven's cloudy hosts
Leading the starry ranks of night,
Sends softly down her banner white,
   Bringing to earth's wide isles and coasts
A blessed truce from noise and strife —
A breath-space for the inner life.

Sweet thoughts, by daylight banished hence,
   Return to comfort and to heal
The weariness of soul and sense —
And on the lips of turbulence
   The starlight sets its silver seal;
Dim pinions fan the fragrant damps,
And fire-flies trim their living lamps.

The dew-born primrose bursts, and flings
   Its perfume in a sudden gush;
Moths flit on silver-dusted wings,
And scores of fair and happy things
   Rejoice in the harmonious hush;

(55)

A bird that dreams of carolling
Chirps faint, with head behind his wing.

By day the city strives and strains,
   And labors in its smoke and dust
Like some great giant bound with chains,
Sore scourged with rods and racked with pains,
   And doomed to servitude unjust;
But when the tiresome day goes down,
The slave may dream of throne and crown.

By day the vulture swoops and feeds,
   And beats his fellows with his wings;
By night all violence recedes —
The whip-poor-will's mild patience pleads —
   Shrilly and clear the cricket sings;
And while the stream its story weaves,
The wind talks softly with the leaves.

If day be storm, and night be calm —
   If day be toil, and night release —
If day be pain, and night be balm —
If day be discord, night a psalm —
   If day be war, and night be peace —
If day be life, and night be death,
Why hold so dear this mortal breath?

Why plead and shudder and bewail,
  When those who stand our souls most near
Slip from our clasp, and, mute and pale,
Recede behind the misty veil
  That hides from us a higher sphere?
Why shrink with anguish and affright
If life be day and death be night?
  Why grieve to see them pass away,
  Since night is sweeter far than day?

KITTY CARY.

No marble tells where Kitty Cary sleeps —
   Only a simple slab of painted pine,
Time-stained and worn, her poor memorial keeps —
   One brief and half-obliterated line —

So near the highway, that the yellow sand
   From passing wheels falls thickly on her grave —
In death, as in her life, proscribed and banned —
   For Kitty Cary lived and died a slave.

Ay, lived and died before the Almighty's hand
   Struck the strong fetters from the bondman's limbs,
And made the farthest borders of the land
   Shake with her dark-browed kindred's freedom
     hymns.

Alas! too early snapped the silver cord,
   Or all too slowly came the tardy good —
Life was to her but toil without reward:
   And death the welcome end of servitude.

Death brought her freedom.   Haply it may be
  That Kitty Cary, from some fairer sphere,
Looks down to-day and pities tenderly
  The bitter bondage of existence here;

Yet smiles to see her race with freedom crowned,
  Subject no longer to a master's rule,
Nor grieves because their thoughtless children bound
  Across her grave-mound, on their way to school;

For nothing guards her humble place of rest,
  The straying cattle browse above her head,
Untended goats pause in their hungry quest
  To crop the scanty herbage from her bed.

Yet Nature's self has not forgotten her,
  But decks her lonely grave with dainty grace;
See! in the wind the blossomed sweet-briars stir,
  And scatter fragrance round her resting-place.

WITH THEE.

IF I could know that after all
These heavy bonds have ceased to thrall,
 We, whom in life the fates divide,
 Should sweetly slumber side by side —
That one green spray would drop its dew
Softly alike above us two,
 All would be well, for I should be
 At last, dear loving heart, with thee!

How sweet to know this dust of ours,
Mingling, will feed the self-same flowers, —
 The scent of leaves, the song-bird's tone,
 At once across our rest be blown, —
One breadth of sun, one sheet of rain
Make green the grass above us twain!
 Ah, sweet and strange, for I should be,
 At last, dear tender heart, with thee!

But half the earth may intervene
Thy place of rest and mine between —

And leagues of land and wastes of waves
May stretch and toss between our graves —
Thy bed with summer light be warm
While snow-drifts heap, in wind and storm,
   My pillow, whose one thorn will be,
   Beloved, that I am not with thee!

But if there be a blissful sphere
Where homesick souls, divided here,
   And wandering wide in useless quest,
   Shall find their longed-for heaven of rest, —
If in that higher, happier birth
We meet the joy we missed on earth,
   All will be well, for I shall be,
   At last, dear loving heart, with thee !

A PINE TREE.

A HANDFUL of moss from the woodside,
   Dappled with gold and brown,
I borrowed, to gladden my chamber
   In the heart of the dusty town ;
And here, in the flickering shadows
   Traced by my window-vine,
It has nursed into life and freshness
   The germ of a giant pine.

I turn from the cool-bosomed lilies
   Dewy the whole day through —
From the flaunting torches of tulips
   Flame-like in form and hue —
From the gorgeous geraniums' glory,
   From the trellis where roses twine,
To welcome this sturdy stranger,
   This poor little alien pine.

Out of this feeble seedling
   What wonders the years may bring !

(62)

Its stem may defy the tempest,
　　Its limbs in the whirlwind sing —
For age, which to men comes laden
　　With weakness and sure decline,
Will add only growth and beauty
　　And strength to this tiny pine.

Hark! is it an airy fancy?
　　The roar of its storm-wrung limbs,
Then the sigh of its tender tassels
　　To the twilight zephyr-hymns ;
The rain on its thick soft greenness,
　　When the spring skies weep and shine —
O, many and mighty the voices
　　Haunting this tiny pine!

Shops, and the jar of machinery,
　　Mills, and the shudder of wheels —
Wharves, and the bustle of commerce,
　　Ships, and the rushing of keels —
Towns, and the hurry of living,
　　The murmur which none may define,
I hear and see as I listen
　　Watching this tiny pine.

I will take it again to the woodside,
　　That safe with its kindred there,

Its evergreen arms may broaden
  Yearly more strong and fair ;
And long after weeds and brambles
  Grow over this head of mine,
The wild-birds will build and warble
  In the boughs of my grateful pine.

TRUE MOTHERHOOD.

ONCE while the Christ walked visibly on earth,
He took the seeming of a little child,
And trod the weary highways up and down,
A poor lost baby, crying bitterly —
His white feet bruised with pebbles, and his curls
Tear-wet and tangled all about his face,
Whose more than mortal beauty had become
     Dim with much grief and crying.

A stately lady, rich and beautiful,
Passed in her gilded chariot, and afar
Saw the poor infant, weeping as he went,
And called to him. "Why weepest thou?" she
     said —
" Come here and I will comfort thee, fair child!"
"I cannot come," the grieving babe replied,
"I seek my mother." And he wept anew,
     And wandered on, still crying.

" Sweet cherub," said the lady, "yet come here —
I am thy mother — see, I wait for thee —

Come! thou shalt be my darling and my own,
Shalt have the daintiest broidered robes to wear,
And silken sandals on thy poor bruised feet, —
And fare most delicately every day;
I am indeed thy mother, lovely child,
    Come here, and cease thy crying!"

"Art thou indeed my mother?" asked the child,
Hushing his sobs a moment as he looked —
"Thy face is fair, and thou art richly clad,
And speakest sweetly — but I fear that thou
Art not indeed my mother — woe is me!
Wert thou indeed my mother, as thou saidst,
Thou wouldst not call to me and say 'Come here!
    And let me soothe thy crying!'

"But thou wouldst haste to bid thy chariot stay,
Wouldst get thee down, and come and take me up,
Wouldst hold me in thy arms and comfort me,
And heal my pain. Ah, no, sweet lady, thou
Art not indeed my mother!" And he held
His mantle to his face and wept again,
And would not be entreated from his grief,
    But went his way, still crying.

INCONSTANCY.

AGAINST the curtained pane, beloved,
  The snow beats thick and fast ;
The wild wind's sorrowing refrain
  Is telling of the past ;
And in the old familiar chair,
  Beside the hearth-fire's glow,
I sit and sing the tender air
  You loved so long ago.

Ah, often since the springs, beloved,
  Have bloomed above your rest,
I breathe the sweet old song that sings
  Itself within my breast —
As children, in the cheerless days
  When winter darkly lowers,
Retrace the garden's sodden ways,
  And talk of last year's flowers.

It never seemed to you, beloved,
  When we walked hand in hand,

Amid the sunshine and the dew
　Of youth's enchanted land —
It never seemed to you or me
　That I could sing or smile
If you were lying silently
　Within your grave the while.

We thought we could not live, beloved,
　If we were torn apart —
That earth would have no more to give
　To either stricken heart ;
Alas, the change that time has wrought !
　Your grave has held you long,
And in a home where you are not,
　I sing the dear old song !

Do you look back to me, beloved,
　From out your happy sphere,
And deem me false, that I can be
　Alive, and you not here ?
Death does not always bring its balm
　To every aching ill —
Life may outlast its dearest charm,
　And heart-break does not kill.

It would have been the same, beloved,
　Had I been first to die ;

INCONSTANCY.

Another love had worn your name,
  More dear, perchance, than I ;
Ah, after all these weary years,
  Would you more constant be?
And would you drop these bitter tears,
  And sing the song for me ?

BRIER-BLOOM.

THE wild azaleas sweeten all the woods,
    The locust swings its garlands of perfume,
But sweetest of all sweets, to-day there broods
    Along the slopes of green and golden gloom
        The scent of brier-bloom.

Sweetest of sweets and fairest of all flowers, —
    A snowy wreath of delicate blossoming,
The blackberry-bramble creeps and hides, or towers
    Above the budding shrubs, with clasp and cling
        Bowering the realm of spring.

Roses are warmer with their passionate red,
    Lilies are queenlier with their hearts of snow,
Magnolia cups a heavier incense shed,
    But when I would be tranced with sweet, I go
        Where the sharp briers grow.

Brave must the hand be, which would bear away
    Their snowy length, and dare the threatened
      doom,

Yet when is past my woodland holiday,
　I can but smile at wounds, and deck my room
　　With wreaths of brier-bloom.

Some souls I love are twinned with flowers like these,
　Recluse, and shrinking from the broadest day,
And full of delicatest fragrances —
　Yet with keen pride to hold false friends at bay,
　　And keep the world away.

AFTER THE STORM.

THE vexed and threatening sky grew calm,
　　By evening's mild approach consoled —
Remote in its dissolving cloud,
　　The thunder farther, faintlier rolled,
And sunset's sudden alchemy changed all the leaden
　　west to gold.

The splendor softened into peace,
　　The warm hues paled in slow decline,
Yet still the waters of the bay
　　Lay golden-bright as amber wine,
While red infrequent lightnings winked along the low
　　horizon line.

Lightly between the sky and wave,
　　A cradling boat swung soft and slow;
Rapt and removed from all the world,
　　Two faces caught the heavenly glow,
And two wide-wandering souls regained the Eden
　　lost so long ago.

The faint breeze slumbered on the deep —
   The few stars trembled in the blue —
   A sacred hush held wave and air,
    As though all loving nature knew
That eyes and hearts and lips at last were utterly and
    only true.

   What eloquence of happy speech,
    What art of story or of song,
   Can reach the bliss of that sweet hour
    When, chastened by denial long,
Love's everlasting patience reaps divine reward for
    years of wrong?

   A tender dawning warmed the east —
    The boat came softly to the shore —
   Labor and care and tumult claimed
    Those hushed, transfigured souls once more,
But nothing in those mingled lives could be again as
    heretofore.

VICTOR.

True, he was not mine; I could not claim him;
    Was he, then, less precious or less fair?
Are we all so selfish and so narrow
    That we love but those whose blood we share?

Ten years since, he was a rare and perfect
    Type of sweet ideal babyhood;
Like a fairy infant, found by moonlight
    In the edge of an enchanted wood.

Like a shining crown upon his forehead
    Lay the soft rings of his amber hair;
Never gentle soul had lovelier casket,
    Never was a mortal child more fair.

Like a lake's calm quiet in the forest,
    Were the peace and clearness of his eyes, —
Full of slumbrous lights and warm, brown shad-
      ows, —
    Dark, yet not forgetful of the skies.

(74)

Then I lost him.   Farther toward the sunset
    Into childhood's active life he grew,
Finding friends in all things pure and lovely,
    Bird, bloom, sunshine, butterfly, and dew.

Child of poets, how could he be other
    Than a subtle poet-spirit, too?
Fine, magnetic, quick to see and follow
    Beckonings of the beautiful and true?

Like a fate, unguessed and unforeshadowed,
    Dropped upon his life its cruel doom,
While the echo of his laugh still sounded,
    And his cheek yet wore its touch of bloom.

At one moment full of life and archness,
    Merry, eager, vigorous, and sweet —
In another, smitten as by lightning —
    Lying lifeless at his mother's feet.

Yet the last faint effort of his being,
    Ere the fluttering life-pulse could depart,
Was to whisper one sweet word of comfort
    To her shocked, despairing, broken heart.

No sharp pang of lingering pain or illness
    Marred his perfect face or thinned his form —

In a moment's space he lay there stricken
Like a lily by a sudden storm.

Who will rightly, in the clouded future,
Fill his place our commoner souls among?
Who will know the truths he would have told us?
Who will sing the songs he would have sung?

A PICTURE.

WITHIN my room's serene seclusion,
  Dwells evermore a pictured face,
Dream-haunted, like a rapt Carthusian,
  With solemn eyes of tenderest grace,
Which seem to compass land and sea,
    Yet never look on me.

O, eyes which gaze beyond and over,
  Yet never meet and answer mine,
What may your steadfast quest discover
  On the horizon's hazy line ?
What charm in yonder distance lies,
    O, sad and wistful eyes ?

Hopeful despite their depth of grieving,
  Still patiently they watch afar,
As though awaiting or perceiving
  The dawn of some unrisen star —
The star which often and again
    My own have sought in vain.

(77)

Sometimes methinks its growing splendor
   Brightens and glows on brow and cheek, —
The eyes grow luminous and tender,
   The lips half tremble as to speak,
And all the face transfigured seems
     By sweet prophetic dreams.

Ah, if when years have told their story,
   Those dreams shall come divinely true,
That dim dawn bloom to sudden glory —
   This face will shine as angels' do, —
These eyes, more dear than angels' be,
     Will look — at last — on me !

DROUGHT.

THE sun uprises, large and red,
  The dawn is lost in a sultry glow;
Like a furnace roof is the heaven o'erhead,
  Like tinder the thirsty earth below;
Hushed is the grateful voice of streams,
  The famished fountains and brooks are dry;
And day by day do the burning beams
  Pour from the pitiless sky.

All things languish and fade and pine;
  Buds are withered before they bloom;
The blighted leaves of the window-vine
  Chase each other about the room;
Vapors gather, then melt in light;
  Rain-clouds promise, then burn away;
And all hearts faint as the sultry night
  Follows the sultry day.

Sadly adown the orchard lines
  The apples shrivel and shrink and fall;

The scanty clusters among the vines
   Wilt, half-ripe, on the scorching wall ;
The peaches perish before their prime,
   The trim espaliers are bare and lorn —
Dry and dead, as in winter time,
   Stand the ranks of the curling corn.

No longer the cool and gurgling songs
   Of warblers freshen the lifeless air ;
The simmering noise of the insect throngs
   Sound incessantly everywhere ;
The ringing rasp of the locust comes
   Piercing the sense like a wedge of sound ;
The wasp from his nest in the gable hums,
   And the cricket shrills from the ground.

The hard dry grasshopper, snugly hid,
   Grates his sharpest, and thinks he sings;
The castanets of the katydid
   Chime with the rattle of sharded wings ;
Blundering, booming, the beetles pass,
   While bats flit silent, as daylight dies ;
And loud in the tangles of seedy grass
   The peevish cat-bird cries.

Open-billed, with his wings a-droop,
   The wren sits silent, and seeks no more

The half-built nest in the sunny stoop,
  Or the children's crumbs by the open door ;
Rustling with dead and brittle stalks
  The paths of the garden are thick with dust ;
And the rows of flower-beds down the walks
  Are baked to an ashy crust.

Parched to blackness the roses die,
  Robbed of sweetness and form and hue ;
Vainly the languid butterfly
  Seeks, as of old, their garnered dew ;
Vain the humming-bird's sweet pursuit ;
  The honey-bee's quest is sparely crowned ;
Happy the mole that gnaws a root
  In his cool nest underground !

The fading foliage of waiting woods,
  The fields all barren and bare and brown,
The city's suffering multitudes,
  The parching roofs of the thirsty town,
The herds which snuff at the yellow grass,
  The leaves which open their palms in vain,
The sea that mirrors a sky like brass —
  All these do pray for rain.

IN PEACE.

Come, let us make his pleasant grave
  Upon this shady shore,
Where the sad river, wave on wave,
  Shall grieve forevermore ;
O long and sweet shall be his dream
  Lulled by its soothing flow —
Sigh softly, softly, shining stream,
  Because he loved you so !

Fair blossom-daughters of the May,
  So lovely in your bloom,
Your ranks must stand aside to-day
  To give our darling room ;
These dew-drops which you shed in showers
  Are loving tears, I know —
Bloom brightly, brightly, grateful flowers,
  Because he loved you so !

Here all the warm, long summer days
  The yellow bees shall come,
(82)

Coquetting down the blossomy ways
 With loud and ringing hum;
While warbling in the sunny trees
 The birds flit to and fro —
Sing sweetly, sweetly, birds and bees,
 Because he loved you so!

Here with their soft and cautious tread,
 The light feet of the shower
Shall walk about his grassy bed,
 And cool the sultry hour;
Yet may not wake to smiles again
 The eyes which sleep below —
Fall lightly, lightly, pleasant rain,
 Because he loved you so!

And when the summer's voice is dumb,
 And lost her bloomy grace,
When sighing autumn tempests come
 To weep above the place,
Till all the forest boughs are thinned,
 Their leafy pride laid low —
Grieve gently, gently, wailing wind,
 Because he loved you so!

And when beneath the chilly light
 That crowns the winter day,

The storms shall clothe his grave in white,
And shut the world away, —
Above his sweet untroubled rest
Fall soft, caressing snow —
Drift tenderly across his breast,
Because he loved you so!

LOST DAYS.

For many tedious nights and days,
  Within this dim imprisoning room,
My soul has groped amid the maze
  Of weariness and pain and gloom —

And as I look abroad again
  On verdant hill, and heavy tree,
And furrowed field, and cultured plain,
  It seems another world to me.

For I have lost the fairest sight,
  The dearest days of all the year —
The sweet beginnings of delight,
  The summer's gradual drawing near;

The new weeds pushing freshly up —
  The eager growing of the grass —
The first ambitious buttercup —
  The maple's morning red, alas —

The first strong throbs of nature's heart,
  When spring her vital magic weaves —

The bursting of the buds apart,
  The crisp uncurling of the leaves.

'T is like a dream of pain and dread —
  I closed my eyes in winter time,
And when once more I lift my head,
  The spring is in its perfect prime.

The wrens which fashion, every spring,
  Their happy nest above my door,
Have taught their young to fly and sing,
  As in all pleasant Mays before —

And I have lost their merry notes,
  Their fearless questions and replies,
The tuning of their joyful throats,
  The querying of their curious eyes.

Along the walk the bushes sway
  Heavy with roses ripe and fair —
The tall syringas all the day
  Sweeten to faintness all the air;

The full-blown clover's fragrance floods
  The land with odor far and near —
Ah! I have lost the time of buds,
  The dearest days in all the year!

FALSE AND TRUE.

Two walked under the olive trees shading the walls
 of an ancient town,
Long ago, as with gold and purple canopied bravely
 the sun went down.

Strangely mated for lovers, they — he an eagle, and
 she a dove —
He with eyes of prophecy, under such a forehead as
 laurels love;

She with bashful and tender face, softly radiant with
 love's surprise —
Flushed with pink, like a peach-tree blossom under
 the fair Italian skies.

"Farewell, darling," he smiling said; "though this
 parting be bitter pain,
To the labor whose crowning waits me I must go —
 but I come again.

(87)

" Then, sweet love, how your heart will beat !   From
    your swallow's nest looking down
You shall see how the eager people greet me back to
    the dear old town !

" Years may pass ere that golden day, fate and for-
    tune may be unkind,
Yet no woman shall call me husband, save the dear
    one I leave behind.

" Will you love me with patient love ? — hold me pre-
    cious the long years through ?
Let us see, when the test is over, which of our two
    hearts proves most true ! "

So he followed his guiding star to the region of song
    and art,
Wrought his dreams in the deathless marble, wooing
    Fame with a lover's heart.

Every shape of immortal youth which the soul of the
    artist thrills,
Charmed to sleep by some weird enchanter under the
    fair Carrara hills —

Gods and heroes of days gone by, saints and cherubs,
    a shining band —

Woke and rose, in their snowy beauty, perfect under
    his master-hand.

Friendship sought him, and praise, and power ; many
    a heart he wronged and rent ;
Many a worship he won and wasted — smiling, spoil-
    ing, where'er he went —

Went the way that an artist loves, skimming the self-
    ish sweets of life —
Giving to no one noble woman, loved and reverenced,
    the name of wife ;

Yet he frittered his heart away, little by little, on
    many shrines,
Keeping nothing for her who, waiting, looked for him
    through her window vines.   .

So his beautiful years went by, charmed by honors
    and ease and gold,
Till at last, after fourscore summers, all the days of
    his life were told.

Then they took him in splendid state, back once more
    to the dear old town,
Where with his early love he wandered long ago as
    the sun went down.

Down the street as his funeral passed, leaning out
from her casement high,
Pale and trembling, a white-haired woman gazed and
wept as the crowd went by.

All are conquered by Fate or Time — there are
changes in fifty years —
Fifty years! and alas, a widow gave the dead man
these burning tears.

She whose youth he had sorely wronged, she whose
heart he had starved and slain,
Now at his tardy coming uttered all her passionate
grief and pain.

Eating the bread of lonely toil, she had waited through
tedious years,
Hoping all things, in tears and silence, fond and
faithful despite her fears ;

Then with a languid, cold consent, after patience and
hope were dead,
Wedded another, whose constant passion sought her
still, though her youth had fled.

Moan of people and chant of priest rose and wailed
like a soul in woe ;

Plumes like midnight, and trailing sables slowly swept
through the street below.

"Oh, my darling!" she sobbed aloud, shaken sore by
her utter woe,
"Oh, my dearest, is this the coming which you prom-
ised so long ago?

"Taunt me not with my broken troth, O my love
whom I still adore!
You who lived in the love of women, winning, wasting
forevermore —

"You who honor the empty husk of your vow when
your lips are dumb, —
No proud woman has called you husband, and you
come — as you pledged to come.

"Loyal to him whose name I bore, yet I loved you,
and only you;
Judge between us, O Mary mother, which is the
false and which the true!"

THE SILENT BATTLE.

The war that Spring and Winter wage
  Goes on in silence, day by day;
Strong youth against decrepid age,
  New growth opposed to dark decay;

The strife of hope against despair,
  Life against death; and morn by morn,
A tenderer warmth is in the air,
  And richer hues and hopes are born.

And lo, on every side appears
  The hurrying host of Spring's advance —
The crowding grass, with bristling spears,
  The brook-side rushes' ready lance,

The javelins of daring reeds,
  The iris-sprout's keen bayonet-thrust,
With rank and file of sturdy weeds
  Rising exultant from the dust.

(92)

Each day a fresher guidon flaunts,
　　Marking the vantage-ground by turns ;
The arrow-heads of water-plants,
　　The hard-clenched fists of valiant ferns,

The willow's pennons, brave and fair,
　　The wild-flag's sharp and slender blade,
With every force of earth and air,
　　Join boldly in the glad crusade,

Till Winter's sullen struggles cease,
　　And cold and darkness fail and flee,
And all the hills are fair with peace,
　　And green with palms of victory.

"UNTIL DEATH."

MAKE me no vows of constancy, dear friend,
    To love me, though I die, thy whole life long,
And love no other till thy days shall end, —
    Nay, it were rash and wrong.

It would not make me sleep more peacefully,
    That thou wast wasting all thy life in woe
For my poor sake; what love thou hast for me,
    Bestow it ere I go!

Thou wouldst not feel my shadowy caress
    If, after death, my soul should linger here;
Men's hearts crave tangible, close tenderness, —
    Love's presence, warm and near.

If thou canst love another, be it so;
    I would not reach out of my quiet grave
To bind thy heart, if it should choose to go; —
    Love should not be a slave.

(94)

My placid ghost, I trust, will walk serene
  In clearer light than gilds these earthly morns,
Above the jealousies and envies keen,
  Which strew this life with thorns.

Thou wilt meet many fairer and more gay
  Than I ; but, trust me, thou canst never find
One who will love and serve thee night and day
  With a more single mind.

Carve not upon a stone when I go hence,
  The praises which remorseful mourners give
To buried wives — a tardy recompense —
  But speak them while I live.

Heap not the heavy marble on my grave,
  To shut away the sunshine and the dew ;
Let small blooms grow there, and let grasses wave,
  And rain-drops filter through.

Forget me when I die ; the violets
  Above my rest will blossom just as blue,
Nor miss thy tears ; even Nature's self forgets ;
  But while I live, be true !

LITTLE FEET.

Two little feet, so small that both may nestle
  In one caressing hand —
Two tender feet upon the untried border
  Of Life's mysterious land —

Dimpled and soft, and pink as peach-tree blossoms
  In April's fragrant days,
How can they walk among the briery tangles
  Edging the world's rough ways?

These rose-white feet along the doubtful future
  Must bear a woman's load;
Alas! since woman has the heaviest burden,
  And walks the hardest road.

Love, for a while, will make the path before them
  All dainty smooth and fair —
Will cull away the brambles, letting only
  The roses blossom there;

But when the mother's watchful eyes are shrouded
    Away from sight of men,
And these dear feet are left without her guiding,
    Who shall direct them then ?

How will they be allured, betrayed, deluded,
    Poor little untaught feet ! —
Into what dreary mazes will they wander ?
    What dangers will they meet ?

Will they go stumbling blindly in the darkness
    Of Sorrow's tearful shades ?
Or find the upland slopes of Peace and Beauty,
    Whose sunlight never fades ?

Will they go toiling up Ambition's summit,
    The common world above ?
Or in some nameless vale, securely sheltered,
    Walk side by side with Love ?

Some feet there be which walk life's track unwounded,
    Which find but pleasant ways ;
Some hearts there be to which this world is only
    A round of happy days.

But they are few.   Far more there are who wander
    Without a hope or friend —

Who find their journey full of pains and losses,
    And long to reach the end.

How shall it be with her, the tender stranger,
    Fair-faced and gentle-eyed,
Before whose unstained feet the world's rude highway
    Stretches so strange and wide?

Ah! who may read the future? For our darling
    We crave all blessings sweet,
And pray that He who feeds the crying ravens
    Will guide the baby's feet.

THE MAGNOLIA TREE.

THE gradual shades of the twilight fall,
　And the scents of flowers, after the heat,
Come freshly over the garden wall —
But one rich odor transcends them all,
　Strong and subtle, and sweet, how sweet!

A wonderful fragrance, deep and rare —
　The breath of the great magnolia flower,
That after the long day's din and glare,
Comes softly forth, like a silent prayer,
　To bless and sweeten the grateful hour.

At morn to the sun's enamored rays
　It opens its bosom's snowy prime;
Pride of the sultry summer days,
It gives its beauty to all who gaze,
　But keeps its soul for the twilight time.

And when the valleys grow dim with night,
　And the skies relent from their noonday heat,
Its long leaves shine in the level light,

And its wide rich flowers of luminous white
    Slowly close, with a gush of sweet.

I see it, glinting in moonlit air,
    With blossoms like white translucent bowls
Of alabaster, all creamy fair,
Filled with a fragrance strange and rare
    As a waft from the land of happy souls.

O gentle airs, which so softly blow,
    Wooing their beauty lover-wise,
Tell me, if haply ye may know,
Is this like the lovely trees which grow
    By the silver streams of Paradise?

For if Nature holds in her gardens wide,
    One thing so perfect and wholly fair
That when we cross to the other side,
Where the green fields smile and the clear waves
        glide,
    We may find it, grown immortal, there —

Safe from winter, and storm, and blight,
    Green and deathless, it seems to me
It is this fair dweller in warmth and light,
With its glossy leaves and its blossoms white,
    The beautiful brave magnolia tree!

Queen of the South and love of the sun!
  Happy indeed must the sleeper be
Who finds his rest, when at last 't is won,
And the dew hangs heavy, and day is done,
  Under the broad magnolia tree!

"HADST THOU BEEN HERE."

OFTEN the simple words return to me,
  Pathetic, sad, yet full of faith sincere,
Breathed by the mournful maid of Bethany,
In her deep sorrow and humility,
    To him she loved so well — "Hadst thou been
      here ! "

For so, O helpful heart, I think of thee,
  In thy continued absence, year on year, —
Saying, when loss or grief has come to me,
And I have lacked thy strength so utterly —
    " I had not suffered thus, hadst thou been here ! "

But ah, in calmer after-thought, I see
  By reason's light, dispassionate and clear,
That all thy love could not have kept from me
The penalties of this mortality,
    O sheltering soul, even hadst thou been here !

For had thy shielding arm encircled me
   Through all the years, and kept me close and
      near,
Still in my treasure moth and rust would be —
Still pain had rent and toil had wearied me,
   And years had aged me, even hadst thou been
      here.

And yet, let reason argue as it may,
   Those words still hold for me a truth most dear —
For though thou couldst not keep all grief away,
Thy presence would have changed the night to day,
   And all been well with me, hadst thou been here!

HUGHENDEN.

THE loveliest day of lovely English June,
   Bright with rare sunshine, crisp and fresh with
      dew ;
   The whole fair landscape seems created new,
And just to live is a delightful boon.
A crystal streamlet pours its tinkling tune
   Gurgling and murmuring its cresses through —
   The velvet greensward wears its tenderest hue,
Dotted with daisies thick as rain-drops strewn, —
And on a sudden from the listening ground
   There springs a living joy, a voice with wings,
   Trailing behind it, as it soars and sings,
A shower of effervescent silver sound —
   A fountain-fall of music clear and strong —
   The bubbling bounty of the sky-lark's song!

TIME'S LOSSES.

IF some kind power, when our youth is ended,
  And life's first freshness lost in languid noon,
Should stay awhile the doom by Fate intended,
  And grant us pityingly one precious boon, —

Saying, " With thwartings, bitterness and trial,
  Your toilsome days thus far have been oppressed ;
Choose now some blessing, fearing no denial,
  To light and charm and beautify the rest " —

What should we ask ? the prize of young ambition ?
  Fame, power, wealth, and gifts of priceless cost ?
Ah, no — our souls would utter the petition —
  " Give us, oh, only give us back our lost !

" No visioned bliss, no pleasure new and splendid,
  No lofty joy by shadow all uncrossed,
No fresh delight undreamed-of, heaven-descended, —
  Only our own — the treasures we have lost."

For wearied out with strife and glare and clamor,
  In time we grow more wise, and clearer-eyed,

No more beguiled by dreams, nor charmed by glamour,
  We dread the new, and love the known, the tried.

And ev'n those lives which hold the saddest story,
  Whose griefs have been most deep, whose joys
    most few,
Have had their raptures, sweet and transitory,
  Their rosy summer-hours of bloom and dew.

Ah, what a lovely group would gather round us,
  Could we but have our vanished back again!
The heart unspoiled, the strength and hope which
    crowned us,
  The bounteous life, the ignorance of pain, —

The plans for noble lives, that earth thereafter
  Might be more pure; the touch of love's warm lip
And saving hand; the sound of childish laughter,
  The peace of home, the joy of comradeship —

The innocence, the ready faith in others,
  The sweet, spontaneous earnestness and truth,
Warm clasps of friends, the tender eyes of mothers,
  And all the sweet inheritance of youth!

We had them all — and now that they have left us,
  We count them carefully and see their worth,

Knowing that time and fortune have bereft us
  Of all the fairest, dearest things on earth.

Ah yes! when on our hearts the years are pressing,
  And all our flower-plats are touched with frost,
We ask no more some new untasted blessing,
  But only sigh, "Oh, give us back our lost!"

FIRE-FLIES.

ERE yet with lingering footsteps comes the dark,
   In the cool chalice of a twilight bloom
Or under some low grass-tuft's canopy,
   The dainty fire-fly makes her tiring-room,
And trims her lamp, and robes her royally,
   With cunning which no mortal eye may mark,
For night's grand carnival, ere long to be,
   With joy and beauty, music and perfume.

Oh, could we walk with noiseless elfin feet
   The rare seclusion where the shining queen
Sits listening to the lovelorn cricket's tune —
   That bashful troubadour who sings unseen —
Making her veiled green bower bright as noon
   With a rich golden lustre mild and sweet,
Yet borrowed neither from the sun nor moon
   Nor any fire, nor ray of star serene.

No legend-lover of the lands afar,
   No story-teller near an Eastern throne,
Who, uttering all his wildest fancies, weaves
   Romaunts and magic tales till night is flown,

So marvellous a heroine conceives
   As this, who asks no aid of lamp or star,
But lights her odorous chamber in the leaves
   With a clear conscious radiance all her own!

When headlong beetles boom across the night
   And high the flowering mimosa tree
Holds its thin flames against the growing dark,
   And heavy dew-drops gather silently —
Up from the grass her mellow opal-spark,
   — A living gem, instinct with joy and light,
Floats tremulous, like a fairy's tiny bark
   Bearing unearthly radiance out at sea.

And then a thousand glitter into view,
   Crowding in fleets, or gathering one by one —
They soar and sink and circle up and down,
   And follow where the airy currents run;
But when the eager day puts on her crown,
   Lo, with the darkness they have faded too —
Stranded like storm-wrecked ships all bruised and
    ϒ   brown —
Their light extinguished and their voyage done.

A WINTER NIGHT.

It was a winter night of stars and frost ; —
  Two friends, with sportive question and reply,
Leaving a cheerful fireside circle, crossed
  The threshold, pausing for a gay good-by.

She speaking lightly, but with earnest eyes
  Telling of grief, or feeling long repressed —
He courtly but severe and worldly-wise —
  A hostess, speeding her departing guest.

She laid her hand in his, with frank farewell,
  And eyes met eyes with smile serene and kind,
When suddenly a clearer vision fell
  Across them — and they knew they had been blind.

Blind in not seeing how their souls had grown
  Dear each to each, all other souls above —
That until now, they had not dreamed or known
  The bliss, the pain, the perfectness of love.

The whole earth might have passed in fire or flood,
   World crashed with world, or systems whirled
      apart,
And they had not perceived it, as they stood
   In that delicious moment, heart to heart.

Only a moment of supreme surprise,
   Delirious joy crushed down by heaviest pain,
And then each conscious soul, too sadly wise,
   Took up the burden of its bonds again.

How could he hope to hide his new-born woe
   Where pleasures whirl and mad ambitions press?
Or in the petty cares which women know,
   How could she look for peace or happiness?

Driven as by a flaming sword, he turned,
   And in the instant, as he left the place,
Into his wildered brain her image burned,
   And all the wordless anguish of her face.

Each trifling detail sank into his heart —
   Even the last year's vine, which stark and bare,
From its supporting trellis torn apart,
   Swung in the winter wind, and touched her hair.

And she, although she kept her quiet guise,
   Nor let the fire upon her hearth grow dim,

Remembered always his despairing eyes,
And knew that all her soul was gone with him.

Each held the secret like a hidden crime,
To be concealed and kept from sight of men —
Yet knowing that the world, nor life, nor time
Could ever henceforth be the same again.

Years passed before the last and darkest night
Closed round his soul; yet then he saw her there
In the cold splendor of the starry light,
With the dead tendrils garlanding her hair.

ADVICE.

HE has told you the same old story
  Told ever anew by wooers —
The story of pure devotion
  Unchanging while life endures —
This passionate, palpitating,
  Persistent lover of yours?

He has called you by every title
  Which lovers love to repeat —
A queen, a goddess, an angel,
  With changes tender and sweet,
And laid the troublesome treasure
  Men call a heart at your feet?

You ask me what you shall answer?
  Ah, child, could my counsel throw
The weight of a thought against him?
  Love never hesitates so!
Answer him No, fair doubter,
  Forever and ever No!

(113)

There lives a marvellous insect
  In the southern meadows far,
Where the wild white ipomeas
  And the passion-flowers are,
That even in broad bright daylight
  Gleams like a living star.

It circles, a flying jewel,
  Beautiful to behold, —
It settles to rest a moment —
  A globule of molten gold ;
But once in the hand imprisoned,
  Its color grows dim and cold ;

You grasp at a flashing jewel
  Worthy a monarch's crown,
Glistening, darting, glancing
  And glittering up and down,
And capture — a sharded beetle,
  Sluggish and dull and brown !

And thus, to a youth's mad fancy
  Is the object of love's wild quest —
Reckoned above all blessings
  Dearest and first and best
So long as remote and elusive —
  But worthless when once possessed.

For weariness comes of having,
  When happiness means pursuit,
And love grows dwarfish and stinted
  And bears but a bitter fruit
When the serpent of self forever
  Is coiling about its root.

So lips which have met in kisses
  Grow chary of tender speech —
So hearts which are bound together
  Grow burdensome each to each,
Since the only things men value
  Are those which they cannot reach.

Who cares for the roadside roses
  Which grow within grasp of all,
While their inaccessible sisters,
  Less lovely and sweet and tall,
But dearer because of their distance, —
  Lean over the garden wall?

So the gainer counts as nothing
  The blessing that should have been —
The conqueror turns indifferent
  From the conquest he gloried in,
Longing, like Alexander,
  For lovelier worlds to win.

Then answer him No, young maiden, —
   Be pitiless and serene;
There are heart-sick wives in plenty,
   But angels are seldom seen;
Keep to your cloud, bright goddess!
   Stay on your throne, fair queen!

YEARS AFTER.

I KNOW the years have rolled across thy grave
    Till it has grown a plot of level grass, —
All summer does its green luxuriance wave
    In silken shimmer on thy breast, alas !
And all the winter it is lost to sight
Beneath a winding-sheet of chilly white.

I know the precious name I loved so much
    Is heard no more the haunts of men among ;
The tree thou plantedst has outgrown thy touch,
    And sings to alien ears its murmuring song ;
The lattice-rose forgets thy tendance sweet,
The air thy laughter, and the sod thy feet.

Through the dear wood where grew thy violets,
    Lies the worn track of travel, toil, and trade ;
And steam's imprisoned demon fumes and frets
    With shrieks that scare the wild bird from the
        shade ;
Mills vex the lazy stream, and on its shore
The timid harebell swings its chimes no more.

But yet — even yet — if I, grown changed and old,
   Should lift my eyes at opening of the door,
And see again thy fair head's waving gold,
   And meet thy dear eyes' tender smile once more,
These years of parting like a night would seem,
And I should say, " I knew it was a dream! "

AT FOURSCORE.

FEW men achieve the life by Heaven intended —
  Few die the late calm death by nature meant ;
Yet with this wintry day is calmly ended
A life which, holding nothing strange or splendid,
  Reached the ideal in fulness and extent.

His was a genial soul, that loved to render
  Kindness for coldness still, and good for guile ;
As buds unclose to meet the sunshine's splendor,
His warm heart opened, flower-like and tender,
  To love's fond touch, or friendship's word and smile.

No loud majorities his praises sounded,
  No proud successes made him eminent,
But children loved him ; all his life abounded
In kindly deeds ; his fourscore years were rounded
  With well-done duties and serene content.

No death more blest could be to mortal given ;
  Love watched the loosing of the silver cord —

And when the golden bowl was gently riven,
Without a pang, exchanging earth for heaven,
  The faithful servant went to his reward.

And though by no proud marble's sculptured masses
  The story of his blameless life is told,
The frozen sods will wake, when winter passes,
And dandelions bright, and tender grasses
  Will broider all his bed with green and gold.

THE VOICES OF SPRING.

SESTINA.

WHY is it that the voices of the spring,
   The bluebird's note, the redbreast's mellow call,
The sweet, sweet carols which the sparrows sing,
   The peeping of the frogs at evening's fall,
These vague regrets and homesick longings bring
   To hearts which listen for and love them all?

All hearts rejoice when winter goes — and all
   Are glad to welcome back the tardy spring;
To hear the woods responding to the call
   Which, rough and blustering, the March winds
      sing, —
To mark the shower's blossom-waking fall,
   And the slight changes which the slow days bring.

And yet, the first soft days are sure to bring
   A tender sadness with their joy, to all —
For with the new growth, buried memories spring
   As once of old at dread enchantment's call,
The dead arose and spake; how can we sing
   Or smile, when tears well up, and fain would fall?

Even the lark's voice has a mournful fall —
　　His lovely golden breast, that seems to bring
The sunshine with it, and the warmth, and all
　　That makes and glorifies the gracious spring,
Is burdened with that long despairing call
　　For one he seeks in vain, — how can he sing ?

We think of strains which hope was wont to sing
　　In youth's sweet Eden-land, before the fall
Did to our souls time's bitter wisdom bring
　　And hush the angel-voices one and all ;
Yet we remember them, and every spring
　　Catch far and faint the echo of their call.

Never does summer-time or autumn call
　　The same soft sadness back ; the birds may sing,
Flowers fade, and ripe October's foliage fall,
　　Yet not the same strange melancholy bring ;
It is the saddest season of them all,
　　The weeping, haunted, unforgetful spring !

Ah, lovely spring ! though mating bluebirds call,
　　And redbreasts sing, and sparrows' song-showers
　　　　fall,
Thy soft hours bring the same sweet pain to all !

ONE OF THREE.

"I AM not quite alone," she said —
  "I have fair daughters three —
And one is dead, and one is wed,
  And one remains with me.

"Awhile I watch, with tenderest care
  Her growth from child to maid,
And plait her fair and shining hair —
  A long and golden braid —

"(Ah, sweet the bloom upon the grape
  Before it leaves the vine!)
And deck and drape her dainty shape
  With garments soft and fine —

"And keep her sacred and apart,
  Until some stranger's plea
With flattering art shall win her heart
  Away from home and me.

"Some lover, in a summer's space,
　　Will woo and covet so
Her lissome grace and white-rose face,
　　That she will smile and go, —

"Leaving her childhood's home and me
　　Forgotten and bereft;
Then there will be, of all my three,
　　Only the dead one left.

"Why count the dead as lost? ah, me,
　　I keep my dead alone,
For only she, of all the three,
　　Will always be my own.

"*She* will not slight, at morn or eve,
　　The old love for the new;
The living leave our hearts to grieve —
　　The dead are always true!"

www.ingramcontent.com/pod-product-compliance
Lightning Source LLC
Chambersburg PA
CBHW030621270326
41927CB00007B/1266